BUILD YOUR OWN
GOTCHA GADGETS
ELECTRONIC GIZMOS TO PLAY 20 TRICKS

BY THE SCIENTISTS
OF KLUTZ LABS

KLUTZ

KLUTZ

creates activity books and other great stuff for kids ages 3 to 103. We began our corporate life in 1977 in a garage we shared with a Chevrolet Impala. Although we've outgrown that first office, Klutz galactic headquarters remains in Palo Alto, California, and we're still staffed entirely by real human beings. For those of you who collect mission statements, here's ours:

• CREATE WONDERFUL THINGS • BE GOOD • HAVE FUN

Write Us
We would love to hear your comments regarding this or any of our books.
We have many!

KLUTZ

450 Lambert Avenue
Palo Alto, CA 94306
thefolks@klutz.com

Manufactured and printed in China. 84

Distributed in the UK by
Scholastic UK Ltd
Westfield Road
Southam, Warwickshire
England CV47 0RA

Distributed in Canada by
Scholastic Canada Ltd
604 King Street West
Toronto, Ontario
Canada M5V 1E1

Distributed in Australia by
Scholastic Australia Ltd
PO Box 579
Gosford, NSW
Australia 2250

Distributed in Hong Kong by
Scholastic Hong Kong Ltd
Suites 2001-2, Top Glory Tower
262 Gloucester Road
Causeway Bay, Hong Kong

FSC
www.fsc.org
MIX
Paper from responsible sources
FSC® C005748

We make Klutz books using resources that have been approved by the Forest Stewardship Council®. This means the paper in this book comes exclusively from trees that have been grown and harvested responsibly.

ISBN 978-0-545-80593-3

4 1 5 8 5 7 0 8 8 8

INSTRUCTIONS FOR PARENTS

- Warning: Only for use by children aged 8 years and older.
- To ensure proper safety and operation, battery replacement must always be done by an adult.
- Use only AAA batteries.
- Hook up the batteries with the correct polarity.
- Keep all batteries away from small children, and immediately dispose of any depleted batteries safely.
- Always remove depleted batteries from the toy.
- Do not short-circuit the supply terminals.
- Battery will overheat if short-circuited.
- If your projects aren't working, replace the batteries with a new battery.
- Do not recharge non-rechargeable batteries.
- Do not use a battery if it is leaking or abnormal in any way.
- Do not disassemble battery or put it in an open flame.
- Possible leakage of electrolyte if battery is abused.
- Rechargeable batteries are only to be charged under adult supervision.
- Rechargeable batteries are to be removed from the toy before being charged.

ELECTRICITY MEETS IMMATURITY

Thousands of scientists and engineers worked over the course of hundreds of years to develop the materials that come with this book. Thanks to their dedication, you can learn about circuits, build your own electronic gadgets — and annoy your family and friends like no one has ever been annoyed before.

THE GADGETS

PUSH BUTTON

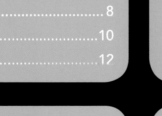

AN ALL-PURPOSE SOUND-EFFECTS MACHINE THAT MARKS LIFE'S GREAT (AND NOT SO GREAT) MOMENTS

MOTION SENSOR

LETS YOU KNOW WHEN SOMEONE MAKES THE WRONG MOVE

LIGHT SENSOR

SITS IN THE DARK, WAITING PATIENTLY FOR THE CHANCE TO SCARE YOUR LITTLE BROTHER

DOOR ALARM

LETS YOU KNOW WHEN SOMETHING IS REALLY AND TRULY ALARMING

WHAT YOU GET

With the stuff in this book, you can build gadgets and use them to set traps, play games, and trick your friends and family. Our ideas will get you started, but once you understand how these gizmos work, you'll think of better ones.

ELECTRONICS MODULE

Big Contact

Small Contact

Mode Wires

Photodetector

Speaker

ALLIGATOR CLIP

Sound Effects

Circuit Board

Battery Holder

LED

AAA 1.5V

GADGET DOCK

PUSH-BUTTON COVERS

DOORKNOB COVERS

DOOR ALARM · PUSH BUTTON · DOOR ALARM · DOOR ALARM

DOOR ALARM

GADGET DOCK

SPEAKER

MOUNTING HOLES

PRESS HERE!

GOTCHA!

WARNING
PROTECTED BY
GOTCHA GADGETS
ALARM SYSTEMS

1. With the speaker on the left side, line up the hooks underneath the electronic module with the blue mounting holes in the dock. Insert the hooks into the holes.

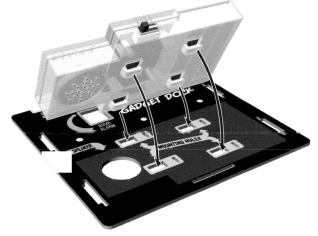

2. Slide the electronic module to the right until it clicks in place.

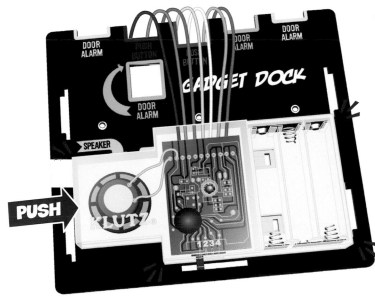

3. Find the purple wire and the green wire and gently twist the metal ends together. Clip the twisted wires with the alligator clip so they stay together.

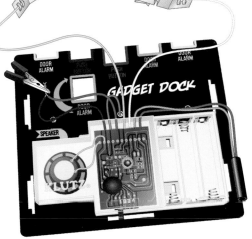

Slip the orange wire through a white hole in the dock for safekeeping. Make sure it isn't touching any other metal.

4. Insert three AAA batteries into the battery holder as shown, spring-side first. Your basic gadget is ready for action.

BATTERY TIPS

- If you know you won't be using your gadget for a few days, take the batteries out to avoid draining them.
- Never connect the plus side of a battery directly to the minus side. That will drain your battery in a hurry.

FUNNY SOUNDS

Transform your basic gadget from a quiet piece of electronic potential into an annoying noise machine.

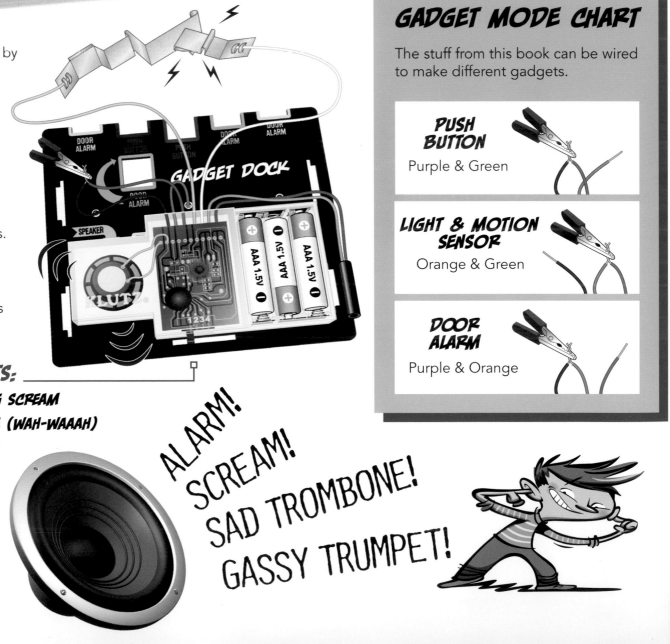

1. Test your gadget by touching the big contact to the small contact. Your gadget will reward you with a startling alarm.

2. Use the sound effects switch to try all the sounds. Each one has a couple different variations, so try them a few times in a row.

SOUND EFFECTS:

1. BLOODCURDLING SCREAM
2. SAD TROMBONE (WAH-WAAAH)
3. GASSY TRUMPET
4. DANGER ALARM

GADGET MODE CHART

The stuff from this book can be wired to make different gadgets.

PUSH BUTTON
Purple & Green

LIGHT & MOTION SENSOR
Orange & Green

DOOR ALARM
Purple & Orange

ALARM!
SCREAM!
SAD TROMBONE!
GASSY TRUMPET!

WHAT DOES THIS HAVE TO DO WITH MY GADGET?

There are tiny particles called electrons moving inside your gadget. A bunch of electrons, all moving in the same direction, make an **electric current.**

Electrons are way too small for anyone to see. To understand invisible things, scientists sometimes compare them to everyday stuff that you can see. Think of an electric current as cars traveling on a one-way street, delivering energy on their way. Using cars as electrons, this picture shows what's happening in a very simple electric setup — just a current flowing from a battery, through a speaker, and back to the battery. This loop is called an **electric circuit**.

The circuit board sends the electric current through different parts of the gadget, depending on how you connect the wires. When that current flows through the speaker, the speaker turns the energy into sound.

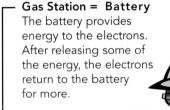

Gas Station = Battery
The battery provides energy to the electrons. After releasing some of the energy, the electrons return to the battery for more.

Why one-way traffic? Because electrons always flow from the negative terminal to the positive one.

ONE WAY

ONE WAY

ONE WAY

Road = Wires
The wires are the roads that connect all the parts of your gadget together. They allow electrons to travel throughout the electric circuit.

Cars = Electrons
The electrons carry energy from the battery throughout the electric circuit.

Alarm Tower = Speaker
When the electric current passes through the speaker, the electrons release some of the energy given to them from the battery. The speaker converts the energy into sound.

We've provided a handy cardboard case. Here's how to put it together and turn your gadget into a push-button machine.

DO THIS FIRST

1. Start by building your basic gadget (page 5). First, slide the small contact onto the dark blue slot on the base, marked "Push Button." Then, slide the big contact onto the red slot.

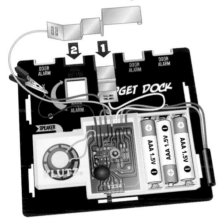

> The metal pieces should stay separated until you press down on the big contact.

2. Bend each side of the case down and crease on the fold lines as shown.

3. Position the dock as shown and slide all the tabs on the case through the slots in the dock. Be sure to put all five tabs through: two on the left and right, and one on the bottom.

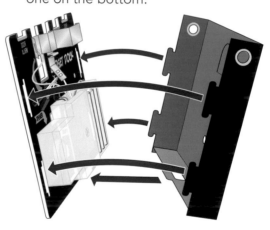

> Push the tabs toward the outside edges of the dock to lock them in place.

4. Test your gadget by pushing where it says "Press Here."

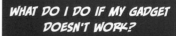

WHAT DO I DO IF MY GADGET DOESN'T WORK?

Turn to page 32 for troubleshooting tips.

HOW DOES THE PUSH BUTTON WORK?

If an electric current is like cars driving on a highway, a switch is like a drawbridge that can block a particular road.

Electricity flows through your gadget's speaker only when the wires and other electrical connections form a complete loop, or **circuit**, starting at one terminal of the battery, passing through the speaker, and returning to the other terminal of the battery.

When your gadget is set up to work as a push-button switch, it holds the two contacts apart. The gap between the metal pieces breaks the loop, so electricity can't flow.

When you push the button, the two metal contacts touch, completing the circuit. The current flows, triggering whatever sound you've chosen.

IT'S ALARMING

Your push-button gadget is like an open-circuit burglar alarm. The switch starts out open, with a space between the two contacts. When a burglar unintentionally hits the switch and presses the two contacts together, that closes the switch and sets off the alarm.

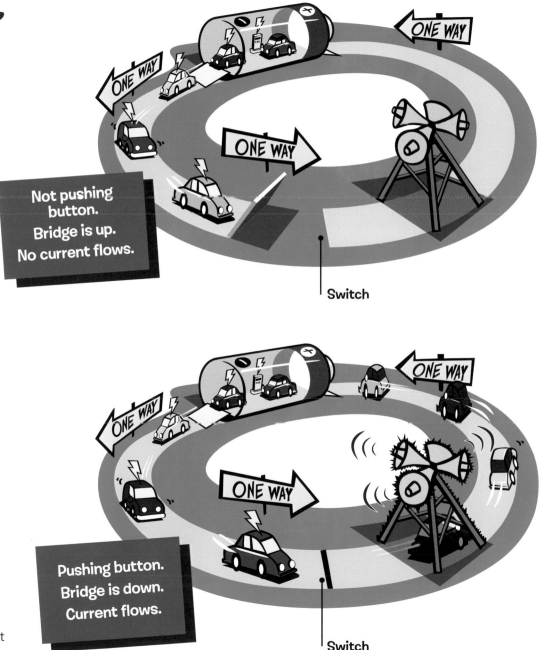

Not pushing button.
Bridge is up.
No current flows.

Switch

Pushing button.
Bridge is down.
Current flows.

Switch

LET 'EM KNOW HOW YOU REALLY FEEL

Have you been holding in your disapproval when people do things that bug you? No more! When you press the button, your gadget can tell the world how you feel.

COMEDY HECKLER

SOUND SETTING: *SAD TROMBONE*

The sad trombone sound cue is known the world over as a sign that someone is comically challenged. Whenever you hear a crummy joke, press the button.

WHEN HECKLING, IT'S GOOD TO HAVE A JOKE OF YOUR OWN READY, JUST IN CASE. HERE'S ONE, FREE OF CHARGE.

Three guys are stranded on a tropical island. They find a magic lamp and rub it. A genie comes out and says he'll grant each guy one wish. The first guy says, "I wish I was back home." Poof! It happens. The second guy says, "I wish I was back home, too." Poof! It happens. The third guy says, "I'm lonely. I wish the other two guys were here."

GAME SHOW BUZZER
SOUND SETTING: *GASSY TRUMPET*

Keep the gadget nearby when you're playing games or watching game shows on TV. When someone gives an incorrect answer, accompany it with a suitable sound effect.

THE BAD-HABIT BREAKER
SOUND SETTING: *SCREAM*

Do you know anyone with a bad habit they are (or should be) trying to break? Help them out. Grab your gadget and follow that person around. The second you see the bad-habit-doer doing that bad-habit thing, press the button. Then say, "You're welcome."

BAD HABITS TO BREAK
(OTHER PEOPLE'S, THAT IS)
WITH YOUR GOTCHA GADGET:

Fingernail biting

Gum smacking

Nose picking

Fibbing

Slouching too much

Not slouching enough

Using poor grammar

Making annoying sounds

NOW THEY'RE PUSHIN' IT

With these activities, the gotchas are right at your fingertips.

DOORBELL

SOUND SETTING: *YOU CHOOSE*

The doorbell serves two purposes: to announce you have company, and to let them know they are entering the You Zone — where anyone can call the shots as long as they are you. Everybody has a front doorbell, but only super-cool people get a doorbell where it's really needed — their room. Choose a cover, pick a sound, and hang your doorbell on the doorknob. Start screening visitors in style.

For this activity, you use a doorknob hanger to cover the gadget instead of the regular gadget case. You put it together the same way (see page 8).

YOU MUST BE **THIS COOL** → TO ENTER THIS ROOM

V.I.P
► COOL PEOPLE ONLY ◄

EXTREME OBSTACLE CHALLENGE
SOUND SETTING: *ALARM*

Your gadget is the perfect endpoint for any obstacle course. The first person to complete the course presses the button and sets off the victory alarm.

OBSTACLE COURSE TIPS

- THINK LEVELS. YOU WANT OBSTACLES AT CRAWLING HEIGHT, JUMPING HEIGHT, AND CLIMBING HEIGHT.

- MAKE A BAR BY PLACING A BROOM ACROSS TWO CHAIRS. SLITHER UNDER.

- TAKE ADVANTAGE OF PREEXISTING OBSTACLES: BUSHES ARE GOOD HURDLES, TREES WERE MADE TO CLIMB, AND SWING SETS ARE PERFECT FOR THE SLALOM (A ZIGZAG COURSE). EVEN CRACKS IN A SIDEWALK CAN SERVE AS MUST-AVOID HAZARDS.

NO BIG DEAL
SOUND SETTING: *SCREAM*

Conduct a (potentially profitable) experiment testing the power of advertising. Here's how: Create a cardboard case for your gadget with a hole for the button, and a money slot. Make a sign that says "Push the button to receive a screaming deal! Only $1!" Draw big arrows pointing to the push button and to the money slot. Make sure you and your gadget can make a quick getaway when your customers realize they've been hornswoggled.

PUSH the BUTTON to receive a SCREAMING DEAL! $$ $ PUSH ONLY $1

LIGHT SENSOR

The gadget that waits in the dark

DO THIS FIRST

1. Start with your basic gadget (page 5). Untwist any wires you twisted together earlier. Then, gently twist the ends of the orange and green wires together. Clip the twisted ends with the alligator clip. Then, slip the purple wire through one of the small white holes in the dock for safekeeping. Make sure the purple wire end isn't touching any other metal.

2. Your gadget is now a light sensor, reacting with sound when the photodetector is hit with light. Test it by covering the end of the photodetector with your finger to block the light. When you take your finger off, the current flows and the speaker makes a sound.

YOUR FINGER HERE

3. Depending on how you want to use the gadget, there are two ways to set up the photodetector. You can leave the wires loose, and snake the photodetector into a hard-to-reach spot . . .

. . . Or you can poke the photodetector through one of the holes in the side of the gadget case, for a more compact light sensor.

When the light is on, the current flows.

WHAT'S GOING ON?

When your gadget light sensor is in the dark, the electric current stops. The electrons inside the photodetector can't move until there's light. Particles inside the photodetector absorb light energy, which allows the electrons to move again.

Darkness turns the traffic light off — no current flows.

WHO TURNED ON THE LIGHT?

To catch a snoop, stash your light sensor in a closed box or bag or drawer. When someone lets in the light, they set off the sound. This basic trick is the electronic equivalent of a springy snake coiled up in a fake can of nuts.

PROTECT THE COOKIES

SOUND SETTING: *SAD TROMBONE*

Put the light sensor into a cookie jar. Tell your family that you've made a batch of delicious cookies that must "cure" in total darkness for 12 hours. How long before a hungry sneak lifts the lid?

DO NOT OPEN!

cookies

SNARE-A-SNOOP
SOUND SETTING: *ALARM*

Place the light sensor inside a drawer along with a note that says "WARNING: You are the world's biggest snoop!" Close the drawer and hide nearby.

FOIL LATE-NIGHT FRIDGE RAIDS
SOUND SETTING: *SCREAM*

Right before bedtime, place the light sensor inside the fridge. When a midnight snacker opens the door, the refrigerator will scream. Race to the kitchen and catch the nibbler in the act. (If you're a heavy sleeper, don't be surprised if you find your gadget in the trash the next morning.)

BOX OF WHAT?
SOUND SETTING: *GASSY TRUMPET*

Hide your light sensor behind a tissue box or any other object in the bathroom. When someone turns on the light in the middle of the night, the unmentionable sound will, um, announce their presence.

LIGHT SENSOR
SCREAM MACHINES

Show your friends how much you care by scaring them half to death.

THE SCREAMER!

FRIGHT BRIGHT

SOUND SETTING: *SCREAM*

THE SETUP

This one is great for a campout or a slumber party. Before dark, untwist the wires and move them apart so they aren't touching (you don't want your gadget to scream until you're ready). Hide your gadget somewhere out of sight with the photodetector positioned where you can hit it with your flashlight beam. When everything's dark and no one's paying attention, twist the orange and green wires together. Now you can trigger it at just the right moment.

THE PAYOFF

Suggest a round of ghost stories. When it's your turn, tell one about "The Screamer." Shine your flashlight onto your face from below to heighten the creepiness. When your friends are on the edge of their seats, say something like "Who is that?" — and point the flashlight at the photodetector. The gadget will scream and your friends will freak.

About five years ago, a series of bizarre murders in this neighborhood had the police stumped. The murder victims had no injuries, but their hair had turned white. They were always discovered with their eyes wide open — as if they had been scared to death.

Don't shine the flashlight anywhere near the light sensor until you're ready.

Witnesses near every crime scene reported hearing a horrible, blood-chilling scream.

After seven murders, everything stopped. No one heard any more screams — until two nights ago, when the eighth body was found on [insert name of local street here].

After interviewing witnesses, police concluded that the screams hadn't come from the victims — they came from the killer. The press nicknamed him The Screamer. The police were hot on the trail of The Screamer when ... Wait ... did you hear that? LOOK OUT!

(POINT YOUR FLASHLIGHT AT THE LIGHT SENSOR.)

AAAAAAAAAAAAGH!

GASLIGHTING
SOUND SETTING: *SCREAM*

THE SETUP

This prank is named after an old movie where a man tricks his wife into thinking she's going crazy. Hide your gadget in a dim spot in a room where your target will be. Place the photodetector where you can hit it with a small, powerful flashlight from wherever you plan to sit. Test it to make sure the flashlight activates the alarm.

THE PAYOFF

When your target is in the room, sit quietly reading a book. Without being seen, quickly shine your flashlight at the light sensor. When it screams, don't react. When the person asks, "Didn't you hear that?" look up from your book and say, "Hear what?" Wait a while, and do it again. Repeat until the target runs out of the room screaming.

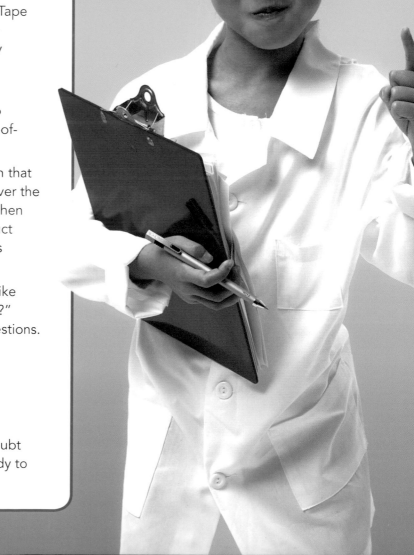

LIGHT SENSOR
THE INTERROGATOR

PHONY LIE DETECTOR
SOUND SETTING: *SAD TROMBONE*

THE SETUP

Attach the Lie Detector cover to your gadget. Then, cut two strips of aluminum foil, each about 2 feet (0.6 m) long and 1 inch (2.5 cm) wide. Tape one end of each strip to the underside of the gadget dock. It's just for show, so don't worry about exactly where to tape it.

Set your gadget on the table and hold the photodetector in your hand, with your thumb covering it. Tell people that you have a state-of-the-art lie detector. Ask for a volunteer.

Have your subject sit across from you. Explain that you will ask a series of questions, and whenever the machine detects a lie, the alarm will sound. Then say, "First, I have to hook you up to it." Instruct your subject to hold the ends of the foil strips tightly in each hand.

Begin the interview with innocent questions like "What is your name?" or "Where do you live?" Then move on to the more embarrassing questions. Whenever you want to make it look like your subject is lying, discreetly move your thumb off the photodetector to sound the alarm.

THE PAYOFF

Watch your subject squirm as they start to doubt reality. (You might want to have a napkin handy to mop up the sweat.)

DO YOU EVER PICK YOUR NOSE?
HAVE YOU EVER SNOOPED IN MY ROOM?
WHAT ARE YOU GETTING ME FOR MY BIRTHDAY?

WHAT'S YOUR
WORST FEAR?
ISN'T IT
ACTUALLY . . .
BUNNIES?!
ARE YOU
LYING NOW?

HOW A REAL LIE DETECTOR WORKS

A real lie detector (called a polygraph) measures physical responses that a person doesn't have much control over: a cuff monitors your blood pressure, electric leads on your fingers detect changes in your skin, and tubes across your chest measure your breathing. When people feel anxious — as they might when lying about important stuff — a polygraph can pick up the silent signals.

POINTERS FOR PRANKSTERS

- BEFORE MOVING YOUR THUMB, MISDIRECT YOUR SUBJECT'S ATTENTION BY LOOKING INTENTLY AT THE LIE DETECTOR (YOUR GADGET).

- IF ANYONE ASKS WHY YOU'RE HOLDING ON TO THE WIRE COMING FROM THE LIE DETECTOR, SAY SOME SCIENTIFIC-SOUNDING MUMBO JUMBO ABOUT CALIBRATING THE GALVANIC SKIN RESPONSES.

- TO KEEP YOUR SUBJECT'S EYES OFF THE PHOTODETECTOR, WAVE YOUR OTHER HAND SLOWLY BACK AND FORTH. EXPLAIN THAT THIS OCCUPIES THE SUBCONSCIOUS MIND, GIVING A MORE ACCURATE READING.

MOTION SENSOR

One wrong move and . . . *Gotcha!*

DO THIS FIRST

1. Build your basic gadget and wire it so it's a light sensor (page 14).

2. Put the gadget in a well-lit area. Wave your hand so it passes over the gadget's photodetector to trigger the alarm.

3. Experiment to figure out how far away your hand can be and still set off the alarm. After that, try to set the alarm off by walking past it.

YOUR PHOTODETECTOR IS MULTITALENTED

The light sensor can also be a motion sensor if it starts off in the light — by detecting passing shadows. When an object moves past the photodetector, the dark shadow quickly resets the gadget. Once the shadow passes, the light reactivates the alarm.

HOW CAN AN ELECTRIC CURRENT MAKE A SOUND?

Put your hand on your throat and say, "Only the shadow knows." Feel that buzzing vibration? That's the sound of your words. Every sound starts with a vibration.

The speaker in your gadget uses two magnets to turn current into a vibration. One is an ordinary magnet that's fixed in place. The other is an electromagnet — a special magnet that only works with electricity — that's attached to a thin plastic cone.

Current flowing through the speaker controls whether the electromagnet is pulled toward the regular magnet or pushed away from it. All the pushing and pulling vibrates the plastic cone so fast that it makes the gotcha sound you hear.

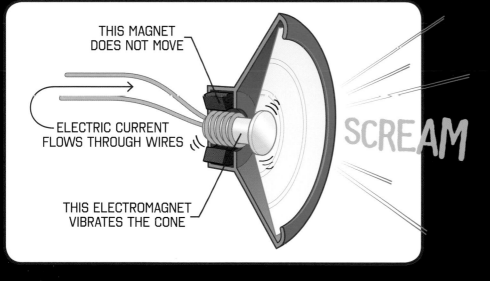

THIS MAGNET DOES NOT MOVE

ELECTRIC CURRENT FLOWS THROUGH WIRES

THIS ELECTROMAGNET VIBRATES THE CONE

SCREAM

CROSSING THE LINE

In these tricks, your gadget acts like a foot-fault judge that lets you know if someone has "crossed the line."

PANIC ATTACK
SOUND SETTING: *ALARM*

THE SETUP

Poke the photodetector through the hole in the side of the gadget case. Set the gadget on the floor next to a doorjamb, so the photodetector points across the open doorway. Then, sit back and wait for an unsuspecting mark to walk in. ("Mark" is con-artist slang for "potential target." An easily pranked person.)

THE PAYOFF

Sometimes the simplest pranks are the best. What's more straightforward than making a loud siren go off when someone enters the room? As soon as your mark steps through the doorway in front of the gadget, they'll trigger the alarm. Just make sure you're ready with an innocent expression and a punch line. ("My Bad Fashion Sense alarm went off! Have you seen the culprit?")

GOOD MARKS

- Someone who's already fallen for other pranks
- Someone enjoying a half-pint of milk
- Someone with hiccups

BAD MARKS

- Someone who can run faster than you
- Someone carrying a stack of china plates
- Someone wearing headphones

EGO BUSTER

SOUND SETTING: *SAD TROMBONE*

Do you know people who think of themselves as big shots? Pick one as your target, and mount the gadget next to Mr. or Ms. Bigshot's mirror. Point the photodetector facing out, toward the spot that person walks past. Every time Mr. (or Ms.) Bigshot walks by, he'll get a nice big bite taken out of his ego.

FIRST ONE THERE'S A ROTTEN EGG

SOUND SETTING: *GASSY TRUMPET*

Invite your friends to run a race, and have your gadget set up at the finish line. Be a good sport and let someone else win the race. The runner who crosses the line first will trigger a triumphant sound effect. Way to go!

SNAP!

SNEAKY STUFF

A motion sensor is a bit like a watchdog — it quietly naps until something gets too close.

THE DINNER WRECKER

SOUND SETTING: *GASSY TRUMPET*

Tape your gadget to the bottom of your target's chair. Tape the photodetector to the very edge of the seat. When your target sits down and blocks the light, it will release the not-so-appetizing sounds.

TIP: Practice your reaction ahead of time, so you can achieve the right mix of disgust and pity.

JEWEL THIEF TRAINING
SOUND SETTING: *SAD TROMBONE*

THE SETUP

Place an object — the "jewel" — in a conspicuous spot. Send your friend out of the room while you set up the gadget somewhere between the jewel and the door.

THE PAYOFF

Challenge your friend to enter the room, snatch the jewel, and make a getaway — all without triggering the alarm. If the alarm sounds, it's your turn. Leave the room while your friend repositions the alarm. Keep switching turns until one of you successfully swipes the jewel.

Good names for priceless jewels:

• The Green Gryphon
• The Eye of Time
• Stargleam

Bad names for priceless jewels:
• The Shiny Wad
• Zeus's Freckle
• Ronald

MY ROOM

DRESSER

CLOTHES

Window

CLOSET

JEWEL HERE

DESK

TOY CHEST

DOOR

Enter through door

MOTION SENSOR HERE?

Be sneaky.
Try hiding
your gadget.

DOOR ALARM

Let visitors know how welcome they aren't.

DO THIS FIRST

1. Start with your basic gadget (page 5). Untwist any wires you twisted together earlier. Gently twist the metal ends of the orange and purple wires together. Clip the twisted ends with the alligator clip.

Most bedroom doors open inward (away from you), with the doorknob on the right side. If your bedroom door is like this, follow step 2 as shown. If your door is different, see page 30 for an alternate setup.

3. Test your gadget by lifting the big contact toward you. When the metal pieces stop touching, the alarm should sound.

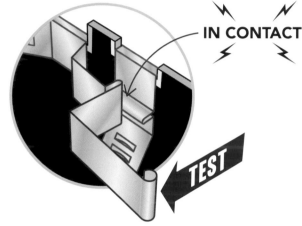

IN CONTACT

TEST

2. First, slide the small contact onto the yellow slot on the right side of the dock, marked "Door Alarm." Then, slide the big contact onto the green slot next to it, facing right.

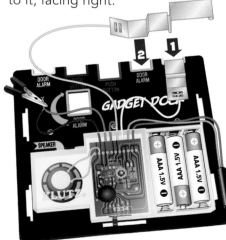

4. Fold the doorknob cover of your choice and attach it to the dock. You do this the same way you made the gadget case (see page 8). Remember to push the tabs toward the outside edges of the dock afterward to lock them in place.

SNOOPER STOPPER

SOUND SETTING: *SCREAM*

THE SETUP

Stand outside your bedroom and close the door. Check that it matches the door in the picture below: The knob is on the right, and the door opens inward. If it doesn't match, see page 30 for an alternate setup. Hang the gadget over your doorknob. The big contact should stick out past the edge of the gadget case. It may take some adjusting, but when you get it right, opening the door will separate the two contacts.

KEEP OUT!
NO TRESPASSING
ENTER AT YOUR OWN RISK

THE PAYOFF

When somebody opens the door, the alarm will alert you. Who will shriek louder — the alarm or your sister?

SETTING THE TRAP

What's going on?

Doorknob is on the RIGHT

Doorknob is on the LEFT

Door Opens INWARD

Doorknob is on the LEFT

Doorknob is on the RIGHT

Door Opens OUTWARD

DOOR TYPE 1

Set up your contacts on the right as described on page 28.

DOOR TYPE 2

(1) Set up your small contact on the left. (2) The big contact attaches upward onto the green hole, instead of along the top.

DOOR TYPE 3

Set up your contacts as described on Door Type 2. Then turn it over.

DOOR TYPE 4

Set up your contacts as described on Door Type 1. Then turn it over.

Create a latch by taping a small piece of card to the door frame. You will need to overlap the contact switch.

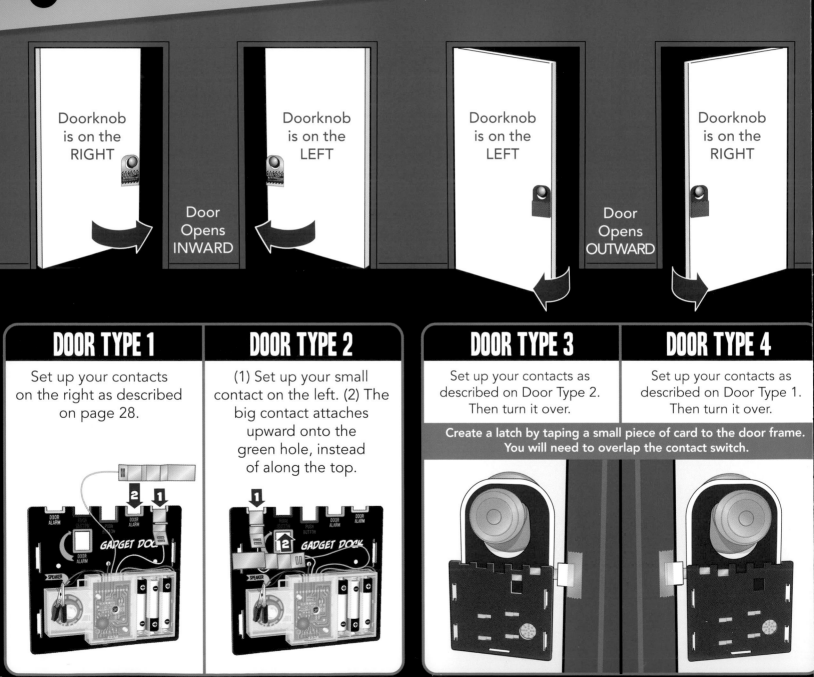

HOW DOES THE ALARM WORK?

In your gadget, an electric current traveling through the speaker triggers a sound. While the door is closed, the door alarm's contacts stay together — making a shortcut that lets all the traffic bypass the speaker. Electrons, like cars, always want to take the shortest route possible. No traffic through the speaker; no sound.

When an intruder opens the door, the contacts separate — opening a drawbridge on that shortcut. Because the shortcut is blocked, the cars have to take the longer route through the speaker — triggering the alarm.

Door is closed. Contacts touch. The shortcut is open.

Speaker

IT'S ALARMING

This type of door alarm is called a closed-circuit burglar alarm. In a closed-circuit alarm, electricity is always flowing. When a burglar breaks and reroutes the flow of electricity by opening a door or window, the alarm sounds.

Door is open. Contacts aren't touching. The shortcut is closed.

Speaker

TROUBLESHOOTING

THE EXPOSED METAL FIBERS IN THE WIRES HAVE BROKEN OFF
SOLUTION

1. Use a pair of scissors to make a very small cut about a half inch from the exposed end. Cut just enough to break the outer plastic casing — don't cut all the way through the wire, or you'll have to start over.

2. Pinch the casing on both sides of the cut you just made and pull it apart, to expose more wire. Then, discard the leftover casing.

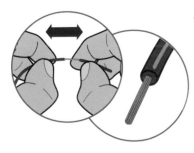

MY DOOR DOESN'T MATCH ANY OF THE DOORS ON PAGE 30. CAN I STILL USE THE DOOR ALARM?
SOLUTION

Wire your gadget so that it functions as a light sensor (see page 14). Poke the photodetector through the hole in the side of the gadget case. Hang the gadget over your doorknob so that the photodetector points toward the wall or doorjamb. Now it should trigger when the door is opened.

THE CONTACTS WON'T STAY ON THE GADGET DOCK.
SOLUTION

The contacts might become loose after repeated use. Tighten them up again by pinching on both sides of their clips until they hold a better grip.

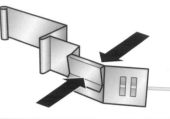

THE CONTACTS DON'T TOUCH EACH OTHER
SOLUTION

Double-check that the contacts are on the correct slots in the gadget dock and are facing the correct way for the gadget function you want. If they still won't touch, they might have gotten bent out of shape. Bend them gently until they match this picture.

I CAN'T GET THE PHOTODETECTOR TO WORK OUTSIDE IN THE SUN
SOLUTION

We can't, either! Sunlight is too intense for the photodetector. If you want to catch someone outdoors, you may need a guard dog*.

*Sold separately